Military Supe...
of th...
Royal Gunpowder Mills

Peter Blake

ROYAL
GUNPOWDER
MILLS
Waltham Abbey

An Archive project of the Royal Gunpowder Mills

Second Edition 2013

First Edition 2011

© Copyright 2013 Royal Gunpowder Mills

ISBN: 978-1492324690

Published by

Royal Gunpowder Mills
Beaulieu Drive, Waltham Abbey, Essex, EN9 1JY
Registered Charity No. 1062968
www.royalgunpowdermills.com

Cover Illustrations

Top: Watercolour (RGM Archive WAI-1248-01) by Peter Jackson
based on the 1735 engraving of the Waltham Abbey Mills published by
J. Farmer (RGM Archive WAI-0093-01).
Left side: Sir William Congreve First Baronet (Philip de Loutherbourg
RA, British Museum) (RGM Archive WAI-0111-01).
Right side top: Francis Torriano Fisher (Official photograph) (RGM
Archive WAI-0054-01).
Right side bottom: Sir William Congreve 2nd Baronet (J. Lonsdale,
National Portrait Gallery) (RGM Archive WAI-0002-01).

Table of Contents

Acknowledgements   5

Foreword   7

Introduction   9

Sir William Congreve 1st Baronet   11

Sir William Congreve 2nd Baronet   20

Thomas Moody   26

Collingwood Dickson   31

William Harrison Askwith   36

John F. L. Baddeley   41

Charles Booth Brackenbury   46

William Henry Noble   51

Frederick Lewis Nathan   56

Francis Torriano Fisher   62

Appendix: List of Superintendents   68

About The Author   71

Acknowledgements

This booklet could not have been written without the help and support of my wife.

I am grateful to Geoffrey Hooper, the last Director of the Establishment at Waltham Abbey, for the Foreword. My thanks also go to Les Tucker, Archivist of the Waltham Abbey Royal Gunpowder Mills for his technical advice and editorial skills; he also selected the illustrations from the Waltham Abbey Images Collection. Thank you to Ian MacFarlane for the layout and design. Catherine Morton Lloyd kindly read the draft and gave valuable comments.

I would also like to acknowledge the assistance given by the staff at the Royal Artillery Archive at Woolwich and the Royal Engineers Archive at Gillingham. My researches also took me to the National Archives at Kew, the British Library and the Guildhall Library.

My key sources were Kane's List of Officers in the Royal Artillery, including the manuscript updates in the Royal Artillery collection and The Connolly Papers, an unpublished manuscript of the service histories of officers in the Royal Engineers kept at Gillingham. "A Short History of the Royal Gunpowder Factory at Waltham Abbey" by W.H. Simmons 1963 was particularly useful for the activities of the two Congreves. A foot-noted version of the booklet and a bibliography will be lodged in the Waltham Abbey Archive.

The Royal Gunpowder Mills acknowledge the generosity of the Gunpowder and Explosives History Group in sponsoring this booklet. The group was established in 1985 as the Gunpowder

Mills Study Group to investigate all aspects of the manufacture of gunpowder. Later its interests expanded to include more modern explosives. In 2009 it became an e-group and donated its remaining funds to furthering the study of the explosives industry through supporting publications by the Royal Gunpowder Mills, where many successful meetings had been held. Back issues of the group's newsletters may be found at:

http://www.royalgunpowdermills.com/history-and-heritage/gehg/

Peter Blake
Enfield
August 2010

Foreword

When I joined the Explosives Research and Development Establishment, the post-WW2 successor to the Royal Gunpowder Mills, the establishment was often referred to locally as the "University of Waltham Abbey". This was indeed justified on account of the high quality and innovative research and development that was being carried out by its scientists and engineers who had the capacity to "think outside the box". This enabled novel technologies to be developed and turned into production processes that could be exploited by the government-owned Royal Ordnance Factories and private industry elsewhere. But this tradition was not just the preserve of the post-war research establishment; it went back many years, certainly as far back as the nationalisation of the powder mills in 1787.

The pioneering work at Waltham Abbey in the late eighteenth and early nineteenth century sponsored by Sir William Congreve set a benchmark in process engineering and quality control that was technically ground-breaking, resulting in gunpowder that was significantly more powerful and consistent in performance than hitherto made anywhere in the world. Also the work on value engineering, cost-benefit analysis and technology transfer to the private sector would not be out of place as a case study in a twenty-first century management course. This tradition carried on at the Royal Gunpowder Mills throughout the nineteenth and early twentieth century, seeing the introduction of new explosives and propellants and the development of process technology to manufacture them both safely and to a high standard of quality and reliability. The safe and efficient production of Cordite was one such example. There were many more, processes for the manufacture of TNT and RDX, still the key ingredients of modern munitions, were to follow.

Throughout its period in government hands, the Royal Gunpowder Factory was also at the forefront of safety management. Indeed, whilst there were occasional accidents at the factory, the overall safety record was excellent, given the leaps into the unknown that were being taken in what was, and still is, an intrinsically hazardous business. Many of the safety procedures put into place at the Royal Gunpowder Factory became the industry standard worldwide. All of this was in no small part due to the qualities of the men that were in charge throughout this extended period. Several were scientists of exceptional calibre and insight in their own right, pioneering those new technologies and procedures which combined process efficiency with safety. This resulted in the Royal Gunpowder Mills becoming the national and international "Mecca" to which producers of explosives and propellants were attracted in order to learn and understand the science and technologies involved. The history of this process development has been extensively recorded elsewhere; what is less well known is the character and personality of some of the individuals involved in the management of the factory who had the imagination, foresight and drive to take forward that science and technology.

This book gives a valuable insight into a number of these men, both at a professional and a personal level, and paints a colourful picture of the role that they played in what was indeed a pivotal part of both the history of the town of Waltham Abbey and of the country.

Dr. Geoffrey Hooper
Head of Establishment 1988-1993

Introduction

These are the personal histories of some of the military superintendents who commanded the Royal Gunpowder Mills at Waltham Abbey from 1787 to 1934. Their stories follow the technological progress of the explosives industry and are also interwoven with the social history of Britain and the Empire.

In the 1790's the industrial revolution was completing its early phase. Factories had been built where a centralised workforce served water and latterly steam powered machines. The canal system was growing. The industrial production of chemicals was in its infancy. The next 150 years would see radical changes. Waltham Abbey began by making gunpowder and it progressed through the chemically based guncotton, cordite, TNT and RDX. It also developed pilot industrial processes for explosives manufacture which were put into production at other sites.

Gunpowder and explosives were manufactured by the State at the Royal Gunpowder Mills at Waltham Abbey under the supervision of a series of army officers. In general it was an officer working a five or seven year assignment as part of a military career progression. On the face of it this is not a promising basis for recruiting the chief executive of a major chemical manufacturing complex and yet Waltham Abbey became renowned for the quality of its product and the innovation of its methods. The officers came from the Royal Artillery or Royal Engineers and they were quite distinct from their brother officers in the line and cavalry regiments. Certainly they had to be accepted as a gentleman, they had to fit in as a bachelor in the mess and they had to be brave. The difference was that the officers of the two Corps were trained at the Cadet College at Woolwich in a strongly vocational course; graduates from university could

9

compete for a direct commission. Promotion was based on seniority not purchase and the rates of pay were significantly higher than the rest of the army. Both Corps were under the Board of Ordnance. The Royal Artillery provided supervision of the manufacture of cannon, gun carriages, small arms and gunpowder, as well as manning the guns. The Royal Engineers were responsible for the construction and maintenance of buildings, factories, fortresses and field works.

The military superintendents received their authority from the Board of Ordnance until it was abolished after the Crimean War. They held various titles over the years; the Congreves were both Comptrollers of the Royal Laboratory at Woolwich. Moody was already Commander of the Royal Engineers at the Waltham Abbey site and on his promotion his title was expanded to "in charge of the Royal Gunpowder Manufactory". In 1840 Moody was made "Inspector of Gunpowder", this title continued until Asquith was made "Superintendent" a year into his tenure in 1855. Nathan became Superintendent of both the Royal Gunpowder Mills and the Royal Small Arms Factory at Enfield Lock, and Fisher also held both positions. From 1934 until closure in 1945 the position of Superintendent was held by civilian chemists in the government service. The final incumbent was titled "managing chemist".

There were 22 superintendents at the RGPF between 1787 and 1945. The nine superintendents in this booklet are those that left a personal impression in the historical record, some for their work at Waltham Abbey and some for other aspects of their careers. One extra officer is included; John Baddeley was the "Captain Instructor" from 1855 to 1860, ranking second in the hierarchy at Waltham Abbey. Baddeley made an outstanding contribution to the manufacture of gunpowder but his early death meant that his full potential was never realised.

Sir William Congreve 1st Baronet

Comptroller of the Royal Laboratory 1783-1812

WAI-0111-02: Sir William Congreve 1st Baronet.
(Philip de Loutherbourg RA, British Museum)

William Congreve was the instigator of the purchase by the Crown of the Waltham Abbey Gunpowder Mills. His epitaph was that "he saved his country a million of money but died unenriched himself."

Congreve was born on 4 July 1742 in Walton, Stafford. He became a cadet at the Royal Military Academy at Woolwich at the age of thirteen, a fire-worker at fifteen and was commissioned as an officer in the Royal Artillery in 1759. In the War of Spanish Succession he served at the siege of Louisville in 1758, which opened the way to Quebec, later he was at the capture of Havana and Martinique.

On 9 December 1771 he married his wife, Rebecca Elmstone, at St Luke's, Old Street, Finsbury in London, by whom he had two sons, William and Thomas-Ralph and two daughters, Anne-Catherine-Penelope and Charlotte. William was later to succeed him as Comptroller of the Royal Laboratory.

Congreve fought in the early stages of the first American War but was wounded in the autumn of 1776. In 1778 he organised the Royal Military Repository, a school of instruction in Artillery exercises and machines. He became Deputy Comptroller of the Royal Laboratory at the Arsenal at Woolwich, (although in practice its acting Comptroller), where the research and development work was undertaken on behalf of the Board of Ordnance.

In 1783, after 24 years service, he had risen to be a major; he was given further responsibility for the manufacture and proof of gunpowder in Britain. At the time of this appointment the government owned a gunpowder mill at Faversham in Kent, the rest of the gunpowder supplies were purchased from civilian manufacturers. Congreve was convinced that the quality of gunpowder could be improved. At the same time the government was being lobbied by the commercial manufacturers that it would be more cost effective to sell the Faversham factory and contract out for the whole supply of it's gunpowder; in contemporary terms that privatisation was better than nationalisation. William Pitt the younger, the prime minister, was going to sell. Congreve submitted his arguments through the Master General of the Ordnance, the Duke of Richmond, to Pitt. His case convinced Pitt to reverse his decision to sell Faversham and indeed to purchase the Mill at Waltham Abbey. In 1787 the run down Waltham Abbey Mills were bought from the Walton family for £10,000.

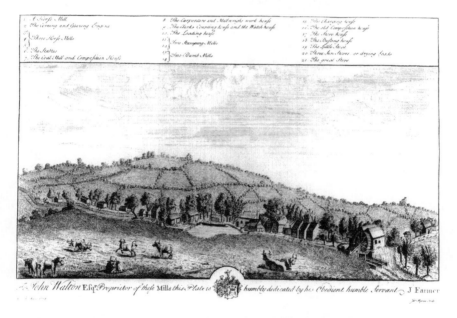

WAI-0093-01: Engraving of John Walton's Powder Mills in 1735 from J. Farmer's "History of the ancient town and once famous Abbey of Waltham from foundation to present time".

In the quest to improve gunpowder each aspect of its manufacture came under Congreve's scrutiny. The purity of each of the three ingredients together with a strict adherence to the mix ratios was a key element. The thoroughness of the mixing and the size of the gunpowder grains were also part of the process. Taken together his reforms were visionary and represented an early example of quality assurance.

The main ingredient of gunpowder is saltpetre, comprising 75%, it was mined in India and roughly refined, then it was shipped round the Cape of Good Hope by the East India Company, and not surprisingly this made it the most expensive of the three elements. It arrived in an impure state called Grough which was about 90% pure Potassium Nitrate. It was refined by a process of solution, filtration, evaporation and crystallization. Congreve repeated this process three times and achieved the highest purity then possible, better than 99.9%. The elimination of impurities helped the keeping qualities of gunpowder, stopping the absorption of moisture.

Charcoal, making up 15%, is the second ingredient of gunpowder; it had been Congreve's special study for some years. The traditional method of making charcoal was to char wood from coppices in pits; this is a woodman's art rather than a chemical process. Congreve had been collaborating with Dr Watson, the Bishop of Llandaff, in experimenting with a new way to make charcoal. The Bishop was actually a Professor of Chemistry and fellow of Trinity College Cambridge. He took no interest in religious matters until after his appointment as Bishop. He seldom visited his diocese and never lived there. The charcoal process that the two developed was based on an earlier suggestion by George Fordyce, a physician and chemist. The new method using a sealed iron vessel gave a completeness of combustion and a consistent quality to the process. It was the new charcoal process which made the greatest difference to the explosive power of gunpowder.

WAI-0261-05: Charcoal Making at RGPF Waltham Abbey.
(Strand Magazine, Volume 9, 1895)

WAI-0101-03: Sulphur Refining at RGPF Waltham Abbey.
(Strand Magazine, Volume 9, 1895)

15

The third ingredient was the 10% Sulphur content which was imported from Sicily. The raw volcanic product was refined by melting and skimming off the impurities and then cooling and crystallising. Two of the surviving buildings at the Royal Gunpowder Mills, the Mixing and the Saltpetre Melting Houses, that were constructed soon after the Government's acquisition of the factory in 1787 reflect Congreve's concern for the preparation of ingredients.

The three ingredients were first individually crushed to a fine powder. They were then mixed together in the Mixing House. The next process was called "Incorporation" which involved a crushing and pulverising process that gave the highest possible homogeneity to the mix; the Incorporating Mill was the first of the "danger buildings". There was a special military appointment of "officer in charge of the danger buildings" at Waltham Abbey which came under the charge of a Captain, Royal Artillery. The incorporated powder was then damped and pressed into a cake. The next stage was to corn the cake into a powder of one of the two specific grain sizes. Finally the powder was dried or "stoved".

Before Congreve took charge the army had settled on a single large grain size. Congreve re-introduced two different grain sizes, coarse for cannon and fine for musketry and priming. This coincided with the move to use the flintlock to fire naval cannon and the introduction of the flintlock rifle to elite army units; the prospect of a misfire became less likely.

Congreve introduced systematic management methods. Written rules covered many aspects of the detail of life in the works. Safety was given a high priority. The elimination of sparks from grit or steel was tackled by leather floor covering, bronze tools, sewn boots and wooden wagon rails. The transfer of powder was made in specially designed covered barges.

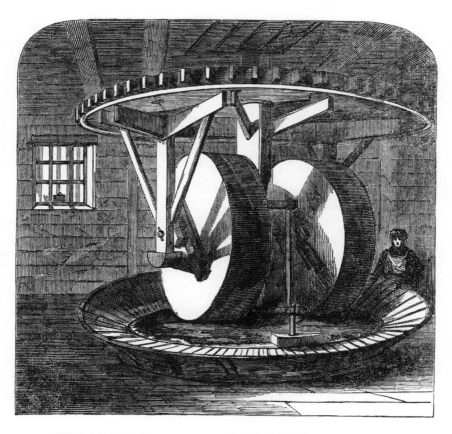

WAI-0448-02: Incorporating Mill at RGPF Waltham Abbey.
(Illustrated London News 11.11.1854)

The results of Congreve's innovations took several forms. There was an increase in the explosive power of the powder; the charge needed was reduced by one third but still gave a better result; gun for gun the British could outrange the French. Gunpowder was stored in barrels each containing 100 pounds and its life in a magazine or a ships hold was short, it could be less than a year in a ship due to the absorption of dampness; to extend the life the quality of the barrels was improved by better supervision of the coopers and the selection of the wood that was used.

The recovery of spoiled powder was an important recycling operation. Some powder could be dried, remixed and re-processed; a very economical way to restore an expensive product. In the case of salt water spoilage only the saltpetre could be recovered and re-used. Congreve brought these processes in-house to get the benefit of the saving; previously the spoiled powder had been sold off cheaply.

There is a carefully costed account of the value of all these changes. In 1811 Congreve wrote his own "Statement of facts relating to the savings which have arisen from manufacturing gunpowder at the Royal Powder Mills and the improvements made since 1783". In this statement he quantifies the contribution that the nationalised mills at Faversham and Waltham Abbey had made.

	£ 000
Saving by producing powder at less than the price that contractors charged	288
Effect of the increase in power of gunpowder	620
Profit on remixing old gunpowder	79
Profit on recovering saltpetre from spoilt powder	31
Profit on issuing purified saltpetre to suppliers over the charge that they make for purifying it themselves	27
Total of savings	1,045

Thus the initiative of one man saved the Treasury over a million pounds.

William Congreve did not himself get rich. He did, however, became a favourite of the Prince of Wales, who made him a Baronet in 1812 and he was still in office as a Lieutenant General when he died in 1814 aged 71. He is buried in the vault of St Luke's Church, Charlton, near Woolwich.

Sir William Congreve 2nd Baronet

Comptroller of the Royal Laboratory, Woolwich 1814-1826

WAI-0002-01: Sir William Congreve 2nd Baronet.
(J. Lonsdale, National Portrait Gallery)

An inventor of genius who died in disgrace.

The second military superintendent of the Royal Gunpowder Factory was the eldest son of the first superintendent and had the same name. Congreve II was born on 20 May 1772; he was educated at several reputable schools including Wolverhampton Grammar School and the Reverend John Tucker's "seminary for young gentlemen" near Gravesend. He was admitted to Trinity College Cambridge where he read mathematics, graduating in 1793. His inherited intelligence and the best possible education produced an inventor of great genius, but sadly he was never quite a gentleman. He did not marry until the last years of his life but lived with a mistress that he had taken over from his friend John Creevy, and he had two sons with her. In 1824 William Congreve married a widow; they had two sons and a daughter.

Little is known of his early career. Congreve may have gone to the Royal Military Academy at Woolwich and may also have read for the Bar at Gray's Inn. He did not join the Royal Artillery.

Unlike his father the second William Congreve was dogged by controversy all his life. He published a newspaper, The Royal Standard and Political Register, which gave outspoken support to the Prince Regent and the Government. The paper lost a libel action to George Cranfield Berkley, later known as "Wellington's Admiral", in 1804 and this ended Congreve's enthusiasm for campaigning journalism.

Congreve turned to invention and innovation. This was to be a continuous stream of creativity for which he is famed. He developed a granulating (corning) machine for the Waltham Abbey Mills, it continued to be used right to the end of gunpowder production and it was probably his greatest technical success; it was praised by Lammot Du Pont, one of the great names of the American gunpowder industry.

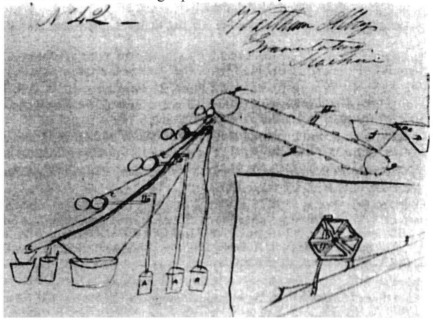

WAI-0561-01: Lammot du Pont's sketch of Granulating Machine at RGPF Waltham Abbey. (Eleutherian Mills Historical Library)

His ingenuity covered a wide range of activities. They included a fire system for the Drury Lane Theatre, a colour printing process, a hydraulic canal lock and a clock regulated by a rolling ball. The most famous was the artillery rocket.

Congreve's rockets and their Waltham Abbey gunpowder propellant and explosive were first used against Boulogne in 1805 and at several sieges including the siege of Flushing in 1809. A letter from a sailor named Wrangle tells the story. The rocket vessel Galqo landed 25 Marine Artillery and 2 officers to assist in the bombardment of Flushing. Wrangle records that when the men were later returned to the Galqo:

"it was truly laughable to witness the impression they made. The practice of discharging the rockets from machines on a ladder was a new invention and proved great injury to the men, burning their hands and faces. Some had no hair on their heads and their hands and shoulders severely scorched".

WAI-0008-06: Engraving showing Congreve Rockets in action at the Battle of Waterloo 18th June 1815.

Another account from the siege of Flushing gives a hint of the feelings of regular officers towards this favourite of the Prince Regent. Richard Henegan was present at the siege and records in his memoirs:

"During that night numerous flights of rockets were thrown from the sand hills, under the immediate superintendence of Colonel Congreve, who stood sponsor to this useful branch of flying artillery, but whether that officer was unacquainted with the properties of these children of his adoption or whether he had arrived too newly from the perfumed atmosphere of Carlton House to relish too close a proximity to the coarser smell of powder I know not; but certain it is that the first flight of these aerial sharp shooters fell in the midst of our own pickets, and did much damage."

Congreve became Lieutenant Colonel two years after this battle but he seems to have had use of that rank in 1809.

On his fathers death in 1814 the younger Congreve took over his fathers post as Comptroller of the Royal Laboratory, and with it the leadership of all the Royal Gunpowder Mills.

Congreve left an account of the improvements that he made at Waltham Abbey. His mixing device was designed to "bring the operation to as great perfection and certainty as possible". Three hoppers, one for each ingredient were mounted in a frame. A cylindrical brush closed the bottom of each supply and revolved to give a continuous flow, the rate of revolution of each brush controlling the proportions of the mixture. A continuous belt carried the mix on to the next machine which, by a series of sievings, took out lumps. This process greatly reduced the dangerous and time consuming incorporating process which used an edge mill. The treatment of the cake was also improved, it being pressed more thinly.

Congreve continued to be an ardent supporter of the Prince of Wales and received much patronage in return, including a commission as lieutenant colonel in the Hanoverian army in 1811, the year the Prince became Prince Regent. In the same year Congreve became a member of parliament for the pocket borough of Gatton in Surrey, supporting the Tory Government.

Congreve was involved in various industrial schemes in his later years including gas street lighting and mining; these were mainly unsuccessful. He was a director of the Arigna Iron and Coal Company. This company failed, fraud was suspected and the case went to court in 1826. Congreve fled the country and settled in the South of France, beyond the reach of British jurisdiction; he died there on 16 May 1828 aged only 56 and is buried in the Protestant and Jewish cemetery in Toulouse. The baronetcy was continued by his infant son; thirty years later it is believed that the son disappeared on his way to the Fiji Islands, he was declared dead and the Baronetcy became extinct.

Congreve's lasting memorial lies in an unlikely place. Congreve's rockets were used in the siege of Fort McHenry in 1812. The sight inspired Francis Scott Key to include the words "the rockets red glare" as illuminating the Star Spangled Banner in the American national anthem.

Thomas Moody

In Charge of the Royal Gunpowder Manufactory, and later Inspector of Gunpowder 1832-1841

He struggled to find his niche in a peacetime world.

Thomas Moody was born on July 16th 1779. He was commissioned as a second Lieutenant in the Royal Engineers in 1806 at the late age of 26. In that year, following the battle of Trafalgar, Britain had command of the sea, and particularly the Caribbean. Moody spent all his wartime service in the West Indies where a small military force mopped up the French possessions in a series of piecemeal operations. Moody's duties were wide ranging, he was wounded twice and helped plan the actions to capture Martinique and Guadeloupe. After the war, and after the restoration of the Islands to the French, the new French king, Louis the Eighteenth, granted Moody the knights cross of the order of military merit for his part in capturing Guadeloupe.

After the war Moody was posted to Ireland, but all did not go well. Some of the travails which beset Thomas Moody can be understood from this extract from the letter that he wrote in November 1831 to his patron Sir Robert Horton, formerly of the Colonial Office, who had moved on to be Governor of Ceylon.

> "From the kindness which you showed me in recommending me to Lords Althorp and Godwich perhaps you will pardon me for mentioning the result. After the pains I had taken to make myself acquainted with the best mode of employing the poor on profitable public works and the practical experience which I have had in the direction and control of labour I confess that I was sanguine that Lord Althorp would employ me as a

commissioner for that object in Ireland, upon your recommendation. I was however, disappointed as he preferred a Mr Radcliffe, who had been about two years in the Corps of Engineers and was very inexperienced. Whilst he obtained a good appointment and salary, Government was pleased to increase my duties and responsibility in the Gunpowder works without any addition to my extra pay of 8d. per diem such increase of duty being for services purely civil, so that at any rate the Government did not think me incompetent. Lord Godwich was also pleased to refuse all my applications for employment; the Secretary-ship of Gibraltar was given to Mr Adderly, a relation of his Lordship. It was on your recommendation I hoped for that appointment. The one in the Mauritius, which you declined asking for, was given to Mr Dick. The Lt. Governorship of Prince Edwards Island on the termination of Colonel Ready's seven years , was given to Lt Colonel Young, who was also allowed to sell his commission. Mr Hay gave me some hope of obtaining this appointment. I equally failed to procure any hope of Van Dieman's Land when Lt Colonel Arthur should be relieved. And the same result attended my hopes of obtaining the combined secretary-ship of Berbice and Demerery, which is given to a young captain in the army. Having, in similar manner, been put off for 4 years, since I was removed by Lord Godwich and having now passed my 50th year, with 7 children to educate and provide for, and my funds saved for that purpose annually lessening, you can conceive what my feelings are of the fairness and justice of the treatment I have received from the Colonial Department and that whatever opinion you may entertain as to the anti Colonial influence to which I have been sacrificed you must admit that facts must naturally lead me to form an opinion anything but favourable of the system which cannot possibly appear to be just in my eyes. Feelings of pride and self respect prevent me giving any further trouble to Lord Godwich.

You doubtless have friends to inform you respecting public affairs and who having better means of information, and more reason to be satisfied, will consequently give more cheerful intelligence than I can conscientiously do. I cannot however avoid the expression of my sincere rejoicing that you are usefully and honourably employed in a remote part of the Empire.

Wishing all health and happiness to yourself and your family, I am, dear Sir Robert,

Yours most truly and respectfully
Thos Moody"

There was an interregnum in the management of the Royal Gunpowder Mills after the departure of the second Congreve, the date is uncertain but he had fled to France in 1826. The Storekeeper, who might best be described as a civilian works manager, continued to run the works on a day to day basis and the Board of Ordnance at Woolwich took any big decisions. There was a Royal Engineer detachment at the Mills in charge of maintaining the buildings and Moody was in charge of it.

At the end of the Napoleonic war production had been running at 25,000 barrels a year. Over the next fifteen years Waltham Abbey was run down to a staff of only 35 men with production of 1,000 barrels a year. The mills became dilapidated and funds were in very short supply, the staff managed to keep at least one example of the components of the production process in good order. The Faversham mills were disposed of and a committee of enquiry was appointed to look at the future of what was now the only government mill left in England. The committee was Col. J. T.

Jones, a Royal Engineer prominent in Wellington's sieges on the Peninsula, Col. Sir Hugh Frazer of the Artillery and Major Thomas Moody. The committee made several practical proposals designed to increase safety and restore production, it also recommended the appointment of an officer in charge to be resident at the site, and in 1832 Moody was appointed to the position.

The shortcomings and improvements included:

> The lack of water power.
> The need to make charcoal on site.
> The need to stagger mills along the mill-head, rather than place them opposite each other, as a safety measure.
> Change from wooden paddle wheels to iron.
> Use of steam stoves rather than glom stoves for drying.

The new superintendent's powers were strictly limited. Each head of department kept his old line of responsibility with the Board of Ordnance. The Commanding Royal Engineer also had independent power and freedom of action over new building. The committee's plan to separate the mills more widely by staggering the buildings on either bank of the mill-head failed for want of co-operation from this Engineer.

In 1841 the census shows that Thomas Moody, aged 60 was living on High Bridge Street, Waltham Abbey, with his wife Martha and six children. Three of these children are given as aged twenty five (this is plainly written on the original document), and the youngest was aged fourteen. The occupations of the two adult sons are given as Army and as civil engineer. He had no live-in servants.

In 1841 Moody left the Royal Gunpowder Mills. He went to Guernsey for two years and then to the West Indies. He designed two military prisons for Barbados. The designs were sent to the Superintendent of prisons who promptly called for a second competing design; Moody's cells had little ventilation and would have been a cruel environment in the sub-tropical heat, the competing design was duly chosen. In 1846 Moody was promoted to full Colonel (Royal Engineers) and posted to Scotland for two years; after that he was he was unemployed. He died on 5th September 1849 aged 70 years at Berrywood House near Southampton.

Collingwood Dickson

Inspector of Gunpowder 1852-1854

WAI-0045-01: Collingwood Dickson.
(Official photograph)

Collingwood Dickson was the most distinguished officer to command at Waltham Abbey. He won the Victoria Cross in the Crimea.

Dickson was born in November 1817 at Valenciennes, France; he was the third son of a British officer and the daughter of a Spanish nobleman. He was educated at the Royal Military Academy at Woolwich from where he was commissioned into the Royal Artillery in December 1835.

In February 1837 Second Lieutenant Dickson was sent with the British Legion to fight in Spain in support of the constitutional party. It was a dynastic struggle for succession to the Spanish throne between the authoritarian Carlos and his niece Christina, who had the backing of the parliament. The campaign lasted nearly three years until Christina prevailed. Dickson returned with knighthoods in the Orders of Charles III, of San Fernando (First class) and of Isabella the Catholic; a good haul for a lieutenant.

In March 1841 Dickson was sent to Turkey to instruct the Sultan's Artillery. He stayed for four years. On his return to England he was promoted to second captain, on seniority, and quickly afterward to brevet major, two ranks higher, on merit. Dickson married Harriet Burnaby, daughter of the vicar of Blakesley in 1847. They had three sons, two of whom predeceased him.

On 1st July 1852 Dickson was given charge of the Gunpowder Mills at Waltham Abbey as Inspector of Gunpowder. It was a time of peace and imperial expansion driven by new technology. The railways were being established in India; new products were exhibited at the Crystal Palace. Gunpowder however had not progressed. Guncotton, or nitrocellulose, had been discovered but it was unsafe. A huge explosion at the Faversham factory led to it being banned. As a result the Waltham Abbey factory which Dickson took over was still making gunpowder with only detail changes made to the methods of the Congreves.

By the beginning of 1854 the dispute between Russia and Turkey had escalated to naval war and the Western powers were being drawn in to protect the Ottoman Empire. The British and French Fleets had been sent through the Bosphorus and full scale war became inevitable. Dickson left the Gunpowder Mills a full month before the declaration of war was made on 28th March. He secured a position on the staff of Lord Raglan, the Commander-in Chief of the expeditionary force destined for the Crimea.

The first major engagement of the Crimea campaign was the battle of the Alma River. The river crossing was defended by large Russian earthworks and the British attack was in the balance. Lord Raglan rode forward to a knoll and called for artillery to be placed there. Dickson brought up two nine pounders and helped serve them. Their fire forced the Russian batteries guarding the coast road to retire. He was promoted brevet lieutenant colonel from that date.

Dickson commanded the siege train on the right of the attack at the siege of Sebastopol. The siege batteries ran short of powder and Dickson directed several field battery wagons to be brought up under heavy fire and helped unload them; for this action he was awarded the Victoria Cross on 23rd June 1855. On 29th June he was made brevet colonel, putting him five years ahead of his contemporaries.

At the battle of Inkerman the next year Dickson brought up two eighteen pounder guns which dominated the Russian guns. He chose the site for them and maintained them despite heavy opposition. When the Russians retreated, Lord Raglan said to him "you have covered yourself with glory". He was mentioned in dispatches, made an aide-de-camp to the queen and received the CB, the Legion d'Honneur and the Mejidiye (second Class). He completed the war with the Turkish forces holding the temporary rank of major-general.

WAI-0448-04: Crimean War scene.
(Illustrated London News 11.11.1854)

On his return to England he visited Waltham Abbey. His death notice in the parish magazine reported:

> "and on his arrival at Waltham Cross Station he met with an enthusiastic welcome from the men who had served under him at the Royal Factory. His carriage was drawn by his admirers from the station to the residence of [Lt Colonel] Askwith RA who had succeeded him as Superintendent in 1854".

Dickson resumed a peacetime career in the Artillery, rising to Lieutenant General on 6th June 1876. He had one more war to go to; he was sent to Constantinople as military attaché in 1877 and served there throughout the Russo Turkish War until September 1879. Sir Collingwood Dickson retired on 20th November 1884, a full general and a GCB. He died on 28th November 1904 and was buried at Kensal Green Cemetery.

William Harrison Askwith

Acting Inspector and then Superintendent, 1854 - 1868

WAI-0046-01: William Harrison Askwith.
(Official photograph)

He modernised the Mills and introduced steam power.

Askwith was born in 1811, the son of a Yorkshire family. He was educated at Woolwich and commissioned in 1829. Some of his early service was spent in Corfu, during that island's short spell under British rule; from there he travelled to Albania and Greece.

Like Dickson, Askwith served in the Spanish campaign against the Carlist rebellion but he was six years senior to Dickson and secured a post as British commissioner to the Spanish Army of the Centre. Askwith spent three years of continuous active service and was constantly under fire; his horse was wounded at the action at Muniesa and Askwith was injured by a spent bullet at La Scenia. His place was at the headquarters and he became friendly with the leading Spanish generals and statesmen of the day. He was made a Knight Commander of the Order of Isabella the Catholic, awarded the Cross of the Order of Charles the III and two Crosses of the Order of San Fernando. His sketches from the campaign were exhibited twenty five years later at MacLean's gallery in the Haymarket. After Spain William Askwith did regimental duties at home and in Jamaica and Malta.

Askwith was selected to be acting Inspector of Gunpowder at Waltham Abbey in place of the departing Dickson who was bound for the Crimea. Askwith was two months short of promotion to lieutenant colonel; both the previous Royal Artillery commanders had been majors. In 1855 he was appointed Superintendent of the RGPF, the first to be given that title; it would appear that the new war needed a more senior figure to ramp up production.

As well as the demands of the Crimean war Askwith's appointment coincided with the beginning of a massive increase in spending at the factory. Les Tucker, an historian of the site writes:

"A whole series of developments took the factory to an advanced state of technology. In 1856 hydraulic press houses utilising water power were built which produced a substantial improvement in pressed material quality and performance. A year later, in 1857, a major transition from water power in the incorporating mills was implemented with the introduction of steam power in the new Group A mills. This was followed successively from 1863 by the impressive range of steam powered incorporating mills on the Queens Mead which forms the centrepiece of the site today."

These mills became the template for gunpowder mill design in Britain and overseas. Additionally, transport within the grounds was improved by extending the canals and the tramway.

Soon after his appointment as acting Superintendent Askwith married Elizabeth Ranken at Abbots Langley in Hertfordshire. The 1861 census records Askwith living in the Superintendent's house at 54 High Bridge Street, Waltham Abbey, with his wife and their four small children. Unlike Mrs Moody ten years earlier, Mrs Askwith had a cook, a nurse, a nursemaid, a housemaid, a kitchen maid and a footman. Eventually the couple had five sons and two daughters. Three of his children were to pre-decease him, one of them died in battle at Suakim. The eldest surviving son became a barrister, prominent in the field of industrial relations and he rose to be Baron Askwith and was knighted.

Waltham Abbey had a triumphal visit from Colonel Dickson on his return from the Crimea. Lt Colonel Askwith's inner thoughts when he saw the be-medalled hero who had leapfrogged him in rank being cheered by the mill workers can only be imagined. However, forty years on, the two men collaborated in writing a paper in the Proceedings of the Royal Artillery Institution on two other distinguished artillerymen.

WAI-0101-09: Hydraulic Press buildings at RGPF Waltham Abbey, with traverse and powder boat. (Strand Magazine, Volume 9, 1895)

WAI-1549-01: Group C Incorporating Mills at RGPF Waltham Abbey.

Askwith left Waltham Abbey in 1868 on promotion to Major General. His active service in the army ended there but he continued on the roll until mandatory retirement aged 70 having risen to full general. His lifetime hobby had been collecting service details of his fellow artillery officers and in retirement this became his main occupation. Kane's List had long been the record of the basic service details of Royal Artillery officers but Askwith greatly augmented later editions, making it a historical record of lasting value. William Askwith enjoyed a long and active retirement, he died in 1897 aged 86 years; he is buried in Kensal Green Cemetery. It is perhaps fitting that seven years later Collingwood Dickson was laid to rest at the same cemetery.

John F. L. Baddeley

Captain Instructor 1855-1860

WAI-1581-01: John F. L. Baddeley.
(Illustrated London News, 1862, Vol XL)

John F. Lodington Baddeley had a short career that had extraordinary consequences.

John Baddeley was born in 1826, the sixth child of a major in the Cavalry. He was a cadet at Woolwich Military academy and commissioned into the Royal Artillery in 1843 at the age of seventeen. His early career included a spell in Jamaica and service as the adjutant of the 10th Battalion.

When the Crimean war began he resigned his post with the 10th Battalion and volunteered for active service. He secured the post of adjutant to the commander of artillery of the Light Division and of the Horse Artillery. Baddeley took part in all the major battles of the campaign; he was at Alma, Balaclava, Inkerman, where he received a severe wound, and at Sebastopol. John Baddeley was mentioned in despatches, he received the Crimea Service Medal with four clasps and he was promoted to Brevet Major. He was also involved in reporting on the Lancaster gun which was on trial.

After the war Baddeley was appointed 'second officer' at Waltham Abbey, under the Superintendent. He was responsible for the introduction of a new way to purify saltpetre. The new process needed only a single refining followed by controlled cooling in flat troughs agitated by rakes. The product had the same perfect purity as the treble refining process and delivered finer crystals; this gave an enormous saving in time, labour and fuel costs. The smaller crystals could be dried more effectively than the larger ones, eliminating more water from the final product and increasing its effectiveness in the gunpowder mix. Baddeley published a paper on the manufacture of gunpowder which described the state of the art at that time including the new saltpetre process.

When the American Civil War broke out the South, with only a few minor gunpowder factories, was in a parlous state for gunpowder supply and a decision was taken to build with the utmost speed a major central factory. There was no one in the South who had experience of designing, building and equipping this specialised structure. Colonel George Washington Rains was the engineer who was deputed to get on with the task. Rains had two large pieces of luck to back up his technical skill, both related to the Waltham Abbey Mills. By this time Waltham Abbey had built up a world reputation for quality and Rains had become aware of and had access to Baddeley's treatise. Using this as a model, even when it did not include any technical drawings, Rains succeeded in creating a major gunpowder complex at Augusta. He was also considerably assisted by Frederick Wright. Wright had been a foreman at Waltham Abbey before emigrating to America and working in a gunpowder factory in the South. Rains heard of him and recruited him to be a valued advisor at Augusta.

After the war Rains freely acknowledged his debt to Baddeley and Wright, albeit enigmatically describing Wright as being 'defective' in a certain way. His audience would have had little difficulty in interpreting this as an over fondness for Tennessee whisky – not the best qualification for a gunpowder supervisor! However his advice seems to have been unaffected. After Augusta Wright advised on local deposits of the raw material for saltpetre and in the course of this was captured by Northern forces, ending up in a notorious prisoner of war camp in the North. Wright survived this imprisonment and returned to work in the gunpowder industry in the South after the war.

Baddeley served five years at Waltham Abbey and was then promoted to Assistant Superintendent of the Royal Small Arms factory at Enfield. He died in that post after a short illness in 1862 aged only thirty six; he left a widow and six children. His funeral showed the remarkable affection that the people who worked with him had for him. The procession was led by 100 of the Royal Artillery from Woolwich and the regimental band, followed by the coffin which was carried on a gun carriage and escorted by three companies of the Middlesex Regiment and their band.

WAI-1548-01: Confederate Powder Mills at Augusta, Georgia, USA.
(Library of Congress, Washington)

Colonels Askwith and Dickson were among the pall bearers and mourners, some 1200 employees of the Gunpowder Mills and the Royal Small Arms factory joined the procession. Three hundred

44

police, both mounted and on foot, controlled the crowd along the route. It was a funeral worthy of a prince.

Charles Booth Brackenbury

Superintendent 1880-1885

WAI-0049-01: Charles Booth Brackenbury.
(Official photograph)

A campaigning reformer for modern military organisation and a champion of gunpowder manufacture.

Charles Booth Brackenbury came from an old Lincolnshire family with a long history of military service. Both his father and his uncle served in the 61st Foot during the Peninsular Campaign, his father was twice wounded, once at Talavera and again at Salamanca. His brother was an artilleryman like him and rose to be General Sir Henry Brackenbury PC GCB.

Charles Brackenbury was born in 1832. His brother Henry went to Eton so perhaps Charles did too. He married at age twenty two to Hilda, the daughter of the Notary at Quebec; they had nine children in all, six sons and three daughters. Two sons joined the Indian Staff Corps and both died in India, one son, Charles, died of typhoid in the Bolan Pass in 1885, the other son, Lionel, died in Manipur in 1891.

Charles Brackenbury was accepted as a cadet at the Royal Military College at Woolwich aged sixteen and entered the Artillery as a sub-lieutenant in 1850. He saw active duty in the Crimea in 1855 with the Chestnut Troop of A Battery of the Royal Horse Artillery where he served with distinction.

Ten years later he was seconded to the Times as a war correspondent during the Austro-Prussian War of 1866 and covered the battle of Königgrätz, a vast conflict with some 450,000 men fighting in an area of less than eight square miles; he came under fire while riding with the Austrian Commander, Benedek. Brackenbury also reported the naval battle at Lissa in the same war.

A further ten years later he again represented the Times, this time in the Franco-Prussian war, observing the Le Mans campaign. In the same year of 1877 he was present at the Russo Turkish war.

He accompanied the Russian Commander Count Gourko in crossing the Balkans in the vanguard of the Russian army to threaten Constantinople. (Collingwood Dickson meanwhile was with the Turks). All in all he had a unique insight into the heart of continental warfare.

In 1873 Charles Brackenbury was attaché to the newly formed Intelligence Branch of the War Office. He read a paper to the Royal United Service Institution (with the Duke of Cambridge in the chair) on the duties of the Intelligence Staff. In 1875 there were just seven officers in the Branch to cover the geography and central logistical planning for the whole of the British Empire. Brackenbury made a case for the expansion of the staff proportionate to that of France, Prussia and Austria.

The experience of the European Campaigns shaped Brackenbury's thinking on military strategy; he was one of the officers influenced by the Prussian army. They advocated open order fighting, rather than line formation and an aggressive attacking style. Other theorists were more influenced by the American Civil War and a defensive stance. He wrote papers criticizing both General Wolseley and his C in C the Duke of Cambridge but, as a serving officer, he could not publish them; instead they came out under the name of Sir Charles Dilke, a campaigning reformer.

Brackenbury became Superintendent of the Royal Gunpowder Mills in July 1880 and held the post for five years. It was the pinnacle of the age of gunpowder. The traditional three ingredients in the usual proportions were given a new form in pellets, pebbles and prisms. The object was to slow the burn rate and to suit the new larger calibre guns; a prolonged explosion produced a continued pressure on the projectile as it was forced up the longer barrel of the bigger guns. He again lectured the Royal United Services Institution, this time on the developments in the science of gunpowder manufacture in a talk entitled "Gunpowder, considered as the spirit of the Artillery".

WAI-0591-01: Pebble Powder.
(Official photograph)

WAI-0590-01: Prism Powder.
(Official photograph)

In the second year of his tenure at the Gunpowder Factory he was living in High Bridge Street in Waltham Abbey with his wife Hilda and three sons and two daughters between the ages of nine and fifteen. His housekeeper was Flora Shaw, sister of his cousin's wife, who had ambitions to be a journalist; she later became Lady Lugard DBE. The census also records that he had three female servants living-in.

After leaving the RGPF in 1885 Brackenbury became the Director of the Royal Artillery College with the rank of Major General. He continued to write on modern European military matters. Charles Brackenbury died of a heart attack in a first class railway carriage between Maze Hill and London Bridge at the age of fifty eight.

William Henry Noble

Superintendent 1885-1892

WAI-0050-01: William Henry Noble.
(Official photograph)

William Noble was an intellectual officer who left a legacy of inventions, manufacturing procedures and safety rules.

William Henry Noble was born in County Fermanagh in 1834; he was the son of the rector of Athoy, County Meath and the grandson of the Archbishop of Armagh. Noble studied experimental science at Trinity College Dublin and graduated with honours.

He was a direct entrant into the Royal Artillery in 1856, bypassing the Cadet College. Within five years he became an associate member of the Ordnance Select Committee.

Noble spent the next sixteen years at Woolwich carrying out experiments in scientific gunnery. He progressed to the staff of the director general of ordnance and then on to the experimental branch. Amongst other things he was on the committee for guncotton, range finding, field artillery and iron armour. He published highly technical publications on the calibre of field guns and on the protection that iron plates give when faced by guns; his papers were dense with tables of measurements interspersed with trigonometry and calculus. He was elected a fellow of the Royal Society.

On promotion to major in 1875 he returned briefly to regimental duties before setting out for the United States where he was to be a judge in the war section of the International Exhibition in Philadelphia. This trip was extended to be a tour of all the United States Army's manufacturing plants and arsenals.

In 1877 he went to India on a tour of inspection of the Indian Army's ordnance factories for a planned re-organisation. While he was in India the Second Afghan war broke out. Noble was given the post of Staff officer of the Kandahar Field Force; he commanded the field train on its march through the Bolan Pass (where Brackenbury's son was to die of typhoid in 1885); for this action he received a mention in dispatches. He caught cholera in India and was never free of illness for the rest of his shortened life.

In July 1885 Noble was appointed Superintendent of the Royal Gunpowder Factory at Waltham Abbey. He was a Lieutenant Colonel, and was soon promoted to Brevet Colonel

William Noble's tenure as superintendent at Waltham Abbey spanned the seven years from 1885 to 1892. Crucially this was the period in which gunpowder reached what turned out to be the peak of its development as a military propellant. It was moulded in prismatic shapes with holes running through. It used charcoal made from rye straw, producing a higher muzzle velocity but at the same time a more even distribution of pressure along the bore, thus avoiding the damaging higher initial pressure associated with solid grains.

Just as gunpowder reached it's apogee along came smokeless chemically based powders which heralded the end of the centuries old dominance of gunpowder as the sole explosive and military propellant. Based on research at Woolwich and Waltham Abbey, Frederick Abel, Chemist to the War Department and chief scientific adviser to the Government, had in 1865 patented a safe and practicable method of manufacturing guncotton. Alfred Nobel perfected the manufacture of nitro-glycerine. At Waltham Abbey in 1888 a major guncotton factory was erected replacing a previous smaller facility. This was followed in 1891 by a nitro-glycerine unit, the two coming together in Cordite manufacture, Abel having patented this material in 1889.

WAI-1496-01: Guncotton Factory at RGPF Waltham Abbey.
(Official photograph)

WAI-0101-20: Quinton Hill Nitroglycerine Factory at RGPF Waltham
Abbey. (Strand Magazine, Volume 9, 1895)

Noble made a novel introduction to Waltham Abbey, it was a boat called The Spark. This small vessel carried a bank of 30 lead acid accumulators. The batteries were charged up by the dynamo at the steam generator house. The boat then proceeded under the power of a small electric motor to a powder house where it was connected to electric lights in safety housings. It was a major improvement over previous lighting methods. The Spark was only allowed because there was no spark.

In 1891 the census records that William Noble was living in Waltham Abbey with his wife Emily and two of his daughters. As well as the family there were three servant girls living in, Minnie, Kate and Florence Risley. Noble had two sons and four daughters in all.

Major General Noble died in office in May 1892 from the effects of the cholera that he caught in the Afghan War. He was just fifty seven. He had overseen the establishment of a whole new chemical technology with all its attendant implications – the commissioning of machinery design (from William Anderson and later his son), the erection and installation of new plant, training of staff, recruiting of laboratory staff, laying down manufacturing procedures and safety rules.

Frederick Lewis Nathan

Officer in Charge of Danger Buildings 1892-1899, Superintendent 1900-1909

WAI-0053-01: Frederick Lewis Nathan.
(Official photograph)

Frederick Nathan was an outstanding chemist and a key figure in the war effort to manufacture explosives.

Nathan was born in 1861 the son of Jewish parents; he was educated at home. He went to the Royal Military Academy at Woolwich and was commissioned in the Royal Artillery in 1879; he was followed to Woolwich by his younger brother Mathew, who joined the Royal Engineers, a third brother, Nathaniel, read for the bar.

Frederick served in India from 1880 to 1882. He joined the Royal Laboratory in 1886, aged 25, beginning a career in explosives production. There were several talented chemists at Woolwich during Nathan's time there. As well as Abel there was Colonel Majendie who later became Her Majesties Chief Inspector of Explosives.

Nathan came to Waltham Abbey in 1892 as officer in charge of the danger buildings, beginning a seventeen year stay. The manufacture of cordite had begun the year before. The cordite process involved manufacturing nitro-glycerine, at that time using German made machinery, and then combining it with guncotton and mineral jelly (Vaseline). The introduction went smoothly until 1894 when a massive explosion killed four workers and injured another twenty. A committee of enquiry could not specify the cause but identified a general slackening of discipline and adherence to safety procedures prevailing at Waltham Abbey; the Superintendent, Colonel Mclintock, abruptly retired.

Nathan was given temporary charge until Colonel Ormsby was appointed. The explosion had wrecked two major buildings and Ormsby's first task was to rebuild the nitro-glycerine facility.

WAI-0031-01: May 1894 explosion at Quinton Hill Nitroglycerine Factory.
(Official photograph)

Ormsby was a man of vision. He was ahead of his time in recognising that new guns being commissioned would have to use cordite; this spelled the end of major contracts for gunpowder and the end of the need for the gunpowder manufacturing capability. Ormsby and Nathan rationalised the layout of the site, with new cordite plant being built in place of the old gunpowder mills enabling a smooth production flow and greater separation between the buildings.

Frederick Nathan found able colleagues at Waltham Abbey. Robert Robertson was appointed to the staff in 1892 and began with a study of the chemistry of nitrocellulose and he was awarded a doctorate for this in 1897; Robertson was then placed in charge of the Waltham Abbey laboratory and made a significant contribution to the investigation of the purification of guncotton. Robertson also devised a recovery method for acetone which resulted in substantial economies in the use of this scarce material. Nathan and Robertson conducted a study of cordite storage conditions which became a reference point for the safe storage of explosives throughout the world.

In 1899 Nathan was promoted to Assistant Superintendent and in 1900 he took charge as Superintendent. In a later tribute Robert Robertson (by then Sir Robert and the Government Chemist), wrote that Nathan:

"contributed notably to the advances then made while at the same time he brought the operative side up to a pitch of the highest efficiency, so that it became the Mecca of the representatives of all the then numerous explosive factories in the country".

In 1906 Nathan was made a Knight Batchelor.

At the end of his posting to the Royal Gunpowder Mills in 1909 Nathan took the post of Superintendent of Messrs Nobel's factory at Ardeer where he was concerned with the devising of stabilisers for propellants. He stayed there until the First World War broke out, at which time he returned to government service. He designed and superintended the construction of the Royal Naval Cordite Factory at Holton Heath. After this he became responsible for all propellant supplies for the last three years of the War. In 1918 he was advanced to Knight Commander of the British Empire.

After the War he joined the Department of Scientific and Industrial Research. One of the subjects that he turned to was the production of industrial alcohol and its use as a fuel for the internal combustion engine. He became the second president of the Institute of Chemical Engineers.

WAI-0443-10: Edmonsey Nitroglycerine Factory Factory at RGPF Waltham Abbey. (Royal Gunpowder Factory photograph album)

Nathan was listed in the attendees at the annual service for Jewish servicemen held at the Synagogue in Great Portland Street. Sir Frederick was a supporter of the Jewish Lads Brigade; he was in charge at some of its annual camps and became its commandant in 1905; he held that position for 21 years.

His brother Mathew became the first Governor of Sierra Leone; he was the first Jew to hold such an office; later he governed the Gold Coast and Hong Kong. His other brother, Nathaniel, became a Colonial Judge in Trinidad. All three brothers were knighted. Frederick Nathan died in 1933 aged 72; he is buried in Willesden Jewish Cemetery.

Francis Torriano Fisher

Superintendent of the Royal Gunpowder Factory and the Royal Small Arms Factory 1909-1917

WAI-0054-01: Francis Torriano Fisher.
(Official photograph)

Francis Torriano Fisher was a Victorian gentleman dealing with the manufacturing and social upheavals of the First World War.

Fisher was the son of a barrister, he went to Harrow School and the Royal Military Academy, Woolwich. Fisher was commissioned in 1882 and served in India from 1884 to 1890 in the Royal Garrison Artillery. Having passed the Staff College course he moved into the administrative side of the Artillery as an inspector of munitions. Later he became an assistant superintendent of the Royal Carriage Factory, and became its Superintendent from 1901 to 1907. He was Superintendent of Experiments at Shoeburyness from 1908 to 1909.

Francis Fisher published two lengthy articles in the Royal Artillery Institution Journal. The first paper covers a device to mechanise the sights for guns firing down from a height; it took advantage of new gun carriage design that remained fixed in place and absorbed the recoil, the sights could be attached to the carriage and needed no link to the barrel.

The second paper covers the training of junior officers in the Royal Garrison Artillery; this paper discusses the on-going education of officers new from the Cadet College. He did not consider that sending them away on formal courses was the answer rather that the instruction of more experienced fellow officers and the experimentation of the young officers themselves were best and they would have hands-on experience of the equipment that they actually needed to master. He doubted the effectiveness of the Gunnery instructors at the school of gunnery because they could not provide gun teams to practise commanding and they were based at headquarters and so only available to a proportion of the young officers. The new officers had plenty of time to train themselves, the working day mainly ended at 11 or 12 in the forenoon; even when on duty the officer is free to leave barracks after afternoon parade, say half past three.

Fisher became Superintendent of both the Royal Gunpowder Factory and the Royal Small Arms Factory at Enfield Lock in 1909. When he came to Waltham Abbey questions were being asked in the House of Commons about the number of men employed and the necessity of the expense. The coming war had not yet cast its shadow.

At the outbreak of the First World War output of cordite had been 26 tons a week. It was immediately increased to 57 tons but in August 1914 orders were received for 140 tons a week. By August 1915 this output had been achieved, and further increased to 200 tons a week. In 1915 the King, with Kitchener by his side, visited the Gunpowder Mills and the Small Arms factories, an indication of their importance. Fisher was made a Commander of the Bath.

WAI-0061-01: Col. Fisher with his Staff. (Official photograph)

In the first two years of the war the factory was using mostly male employees, as war workers the staff had exemption from enlistment. By 1915 the nation was creating a civilian army to break the stalemate on the Western Front and the policy for exempt workers was changed. Women were to be recruited in place of men fit for service. The process was called "combing-out". In May 1916 it was announced that 4,000 women were to be taken on at the RGPF, the Royal Small Arms Factory and other munitions works in the area.

Fisher responded promptly to the challenge of a regiment of women. He decided to recruit a woman at a senior level to be the supervisor of the new female work force. His appointee was Hilda Walton, a graduate of independent mind and firm resolve. She resigned after two months, saying that there were only forty women on the payroll and no prospect of increasing the numbers; furthermore there was no suitable accommodation even if the situation changed. Fisher appealed to her to re-consider but Hilda stuck to her guns, perhaps because Fisher had lodged her in the women's shifting room. The qualities required of a lady superintendent are shown by Hilda's successor, Miss Jean O'Brien, who had been Lady Superintendent at University College Hospital, and later organised training for a division of the British Red Cross; her qualifications and experience included nursing, accountancy, social work, lecturing and clerical work. In due course 3,000 women were employed along with 2,000 men that remained. The site at Waltham Abbey was extended and new cordite works were built.

The Zeppelin raids were a threat. An airship was shot down over Potters Bar, not far away to the west. With the Gunpowder Mills within range of enemy bombs it is surprising that Waltham Abbey remained in the business of explosives manufacture for so long afterwards; in fact well into World War II. A "lights out" was ordered for a one mile radius round Waltham Abbey Church

In the darkened streets the wife of a RGPF worker went to the factory to deliver a medical certificate for her husband, she fell into the river and was drowned; a week later another local walked into the river and drowned. There were four other deaths by drowning around Waltham Abbey in the stormy winter of 1915, but the blackout was not cited as a cause. Fisher himself added to the accident statistics by running over a pedestrian while driving his car in the area.

WAI-0443-29: Women workers at RGPF Waltham Abbey in WWI, 1917 showing range of protective clothing worn. (Royal Gunpowder Factory photograph album)

The record of the Mills throughout the First World War was outstanding, reflecting credit on all concerned – Fisher and his successor, the 3000 ladies who were suddenly snatched from the domestic life to the very different environment of a munitions factory, the officers who oversaw the danger buildings and the management and supervisory staff and male workers who remained at the Factory. The production of explosives is a hazardous business. Throughout the war the Factory suffered only one serious accident, which in relation to the production environment and the record of other ostensibly safer industries was a remarkable achievement.

Colonel Fisher left the Waltham Abbey and Enfield Factories in 1917 and, it would appear, he retired. The newspapers have no further record of his activities until he died in 1938 in Sevenoaks, Kent aged 75.

Appendix: List of Superintendents

List of Superintendents, Storekeepers, and Inspectors of Gunpowder at the Royal Gunpowder Mills, Waltham Abbey.

Date Start	Date End	Name
		(* in Military Superintendents book)
1779	1787	* Captain Sir William Congreve, 1st Baronet. Comptroller of the Mills. First person responsible for the site prior to purchase by the Government. Involved with improving production techniques until 09/02/1789. (1787-1812?)
11/10/1787	1805	Mr James Wright (1). Appointed Storekeeper responsible for the site after purchase by the Government.
06/04/1805	1818	Mr H S Matthews. Appointed Storekeeper responsible for the site.
1814	1826	* Lieutenant Colonel Sir William Congreve, 2nd Baronet. Comptroller of the Mills. (succeeded his father, 1st Baronet)
20/01/1818	17/06/1825	Mr E Middleton. Appointed Storekeeper responsible for the site. (died 17/06/1825)
29/06/1825	14/10/1831	Mr C Wilks. Appointed Storekeeper responsible for the site.
15/10/1831	1832	Mr James Wright (2) appointed Deputy Storekeeper responsible for the site.
13/10/1832	01/07/1840	* Lieutenant Colonel C T Moody CRE. In charge of the Royal Gunpowder Manufactory.
02/07/1840	1845	* Lieutenant Colonel C T Moody CRE. Inspector of Gunpowder responsible for the site.
27/11/1845	30/06/1852	Captain Alexander T Tulloh RA. Inspector of Gunpowder responsible for the site.
01/07/1852	14/02/1854	* Major C Collingwood Dickson RA. Inspector of Gunpowder responsible for the site.
02/1854	03/1854	Capt W Henderson RA. Acting Inspector of Gunpowder responsible for the site.
04/1854	1855	* Colonel William Harrison Askwith RA. Acting Inspector of Gunpowder responsible for the site.

18/08/1855	26/02/1868	* Colonel William Harrison Askwith RA. Appointed Superintendent responsible for the site. The first to be given the title Superintendent.
27/02/1868	31/03/1875	Colonel C W Younghusband RA. Appointed Superintendent responsible for the site.
01/04/1875	25/05/1875	Lieutenant Colonel Young RA. Appointed Superintendent responsible for the site. (died 25/05/1875).
26/05/1875	28/06/1875	Captain Morgan RA. Appointed Acting Superintendent responsible for the site.
29/06/1875	30/06/1880	Colonel Robert J Hay KCB. Appointed Superintendent responsible for the site.
01/07/1880	30/06/1885	* Colonel C B BrackenburyRA. Appointed Superintendent responsible for the site.
01/07/1885	17/05/1892	* Major General W H Noble. Appointed Superintendent responsible for the site. (died 17/05/1892)
01/04/1892	30/09/1892	Major F W J Barker RA. Appointed Acting Superintendent during Major General Noble's illness.
01/10/1892	13/07/1894	Lieutenant Colonel W McClintock RA. Appointed Superintendent responsible for the site.
31/05/1894	26/07/1894	Major Frederick Lewis Nathan RA. Appointed Acting Superintendent responsible for the site.
27/07/1894	20/01/1900	Colonel J B Ormsby. Appointed Superintendent responsible for the site.
21/01/1900	04/08/1909	* Bt Colonel Sir Frederick L Nathan Knt RA. Appointed Superintendent responsible for the site. Later appointed Superintendent responsible for the RG & SA Factories - 08/02/1909 to 04/08/1909.
06/08/1909	14/12/1917	* Major Francis Torriano Fisher RA. Appointed Superintendent responsible for the RG & SA Factories.
15/12/1917	11/07/1934	Lieutenant Colonel P H Evans RA. Appointed Superintendent responsible for the site.
12/07/1934	31/07/1939	Dr R C Bowden OBE PhD MSc FIC MI ChemE FCS. First civilian to be appointed Superintendent responsible for the site. Beginning of winding down of RGPF.

01/08/1939	31/12/1943	Mr P G Knapman MBE BSc FIC. Appointed Superintendent responsible for the site. Later, ADOF 1944-1950.
01/01/1944	28/07/1945	Mr R F Smith BSc ARIC AMI ChemE. Apopointeed Managing Chemist responsible for the site until formal closure as an Ordnance Factory on 28/07/1945.
1945	1946	Dr F J Wilkins. Chief Superintendent of CRDD.
1946	1949	Dr H J Poole CBE. Chief Superintendent of ERDE.
1950	1954	Dr C H Johnson CBE. Chief Superintendent of ERDE.
07/1954	12/1957	Mr L T D Williams CMG. Director of ERDE.
01/1958	05/1959	Mr A Brewin OBE. Acting Director of ERDE.
01/06/1959	12/11/1959	Mr W H Wheeler CMG. Director of ERDE.
1959	1964	Dr C H Johnson CBE. Director of ERDE.
06/1964	09/1976	Dr L J. Bellamy CBE. Director of ERDE.
10/1976	05/1980	Dr F H Panton MBE. Director of PERME. Head of RME.
07/1980	03/1984	Dr B H Newman. Director of PERME. Head of RME.
1984	1988	Dr Alan J Owen. Director.
03/1988	06/1991	* Dr Geoffrey Hooper. Director until June 1991 when the site formally closed.

About The Author

Peter Blake spent his working life as a Chartered Accountant, latterly in the Charity sector, but had a long term interest in naval and military history. While still working he attended the summer school of the Greenwich Maritime Institute in 2005, the anniversary of the Battle of Trafalgar; this triggered a desire to take a hands-on involvement with historical research.

After retiring he took a Masters degree in Maritime History at the Greenwich Maritime Institute. His dissertation was on the siege of Flushing in 1809 where the second Sir William Congreve, who features in this booklet, brought his rockets to bear. The Archive section of the Royal Gunpowder Mills gave Peter Blake the opportunity to take on this project, for which he is very grateful.

8189853R00042

Printed in Great Britain
by Amazon.co.uk, Ltd.,
Marston Gate.